HAL•LEONARD
INSTRUMENTAL
PLAY-ALONG

AUDIO
ACCESS
INCLUDED

PLAYBACK+
Speed • Pitch • Balance • Loop

TRUMPET

CONTEMPORARY
BROADWAY

T0081864

Audio arrangements by Peter Deneff

To access audio, visit:
www.halleonard.com/mylibrary

Enter Code
1267-9571-6740-0726

ISBN 978-1-5400-5929-1

Visit Hal Leonard Online at
www.halleonard.com

Contact us:
Hal Leonard
7777 West Bluemound Road
Milwaukee, WI 53213
Email: info@halleonard.com

In Europe, contact:
Hal Leonard Europe Limited
42 Wigmore Street
Marylebone, London, W1U 2RN
Email: info@halleonardeurope.com

In Australia, contact:
Hal Leonard Australia Pty. Ltd.
4 Lentara Court
Cheltenham, Victoria, 3192 Australia
Email: info@halleonard.com.au

CONTENTS

4

ALL THAT MATTERS

from FINDING NEVERLAND

TRUMPET

Words and Music by ELIOT KENNEDY
and GARY BARLOW

DEFYING GRAVITY
from the Broadway Musical WICKED

TRUMPET

Music and Lyrics by
STEPHEN SCHWARTZ

ME AND THE SKY

from COME FROM AWAY

TRUMPET

Music and Lyrics by IRENE SANKOFF
and DAVID HEIN

MICHAEL IN THE BATHROOM

from BE MORE CHILL

TRUMPET

Words and Music by
JOE ICONIS

MY SHOT
from HAMILTON

TRUMPET

Words and Music by LIN-MANUEL MIRANDA
with ALBERT JOHNSON, KEJUAN WALIEK MUCHITA,
OSTON HARVEY, JR., ROGER TROUTMAN,
CHRISTOPHER WALLACE

ONCE UPON A DECEMBER

from the Broadway Musical ANASTASIA

TRUMPET

Words and Music by LYNN AHRENS
and STEPHEN FLAHERTY

PRACTICALLY PERFECT

from MARY POPPINS

TRUMPET

Music by GEORGE STILES
Lyrics by ANTHONY DREWE

PROUD OF YOUR BOY
from ALADDIN

TRUMPET

Music by ALAN MENKEN
Lyrics by HOWARD ASHMAN

RIGHT HAND MAN
from SOMETHING ROTTEN!

TRUMPET

Words and Music by WAYNE KIRKPATRICK
and KAREY KIRKPATRICK

19

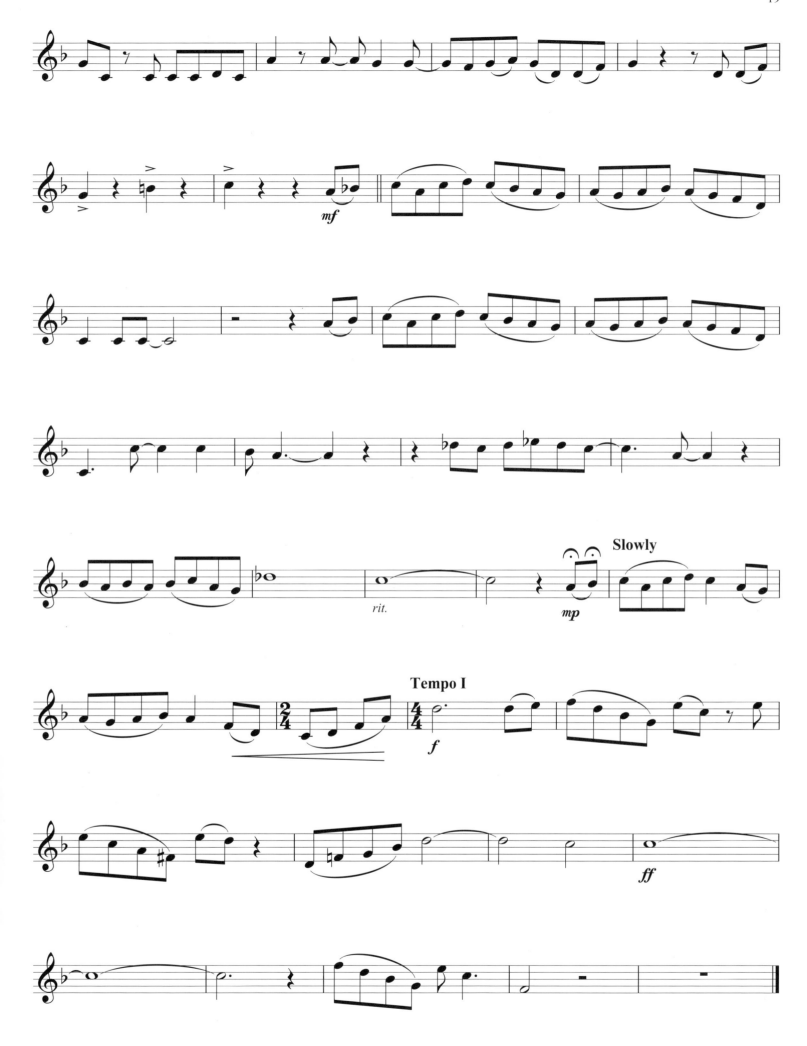

SEIZE THE DAY
from NEWSIES THE MUSICAL

TRUMPET

Music by ALAN MENKEN
Lyrics by JACK FELDMAN

SHE USED TO BE MINE

from WAITRESS

TRUMPET

Words and Music by
SARA BAREILLES

23

STUPID WITH LOVE

from MEAN GIRLS

Words by NELL BENJAMIN
Music by JEFFREY RICHMOND

TRUMPET

D.S. al Coda

CODA

WAVING THROUGH A WINDOW
from DEAR EVAN HANSEN

TRUMPET

Music and Lyrics by BENJ PASEK
and JUSTIN PAUL

CODA

WHEN I GROW UP

from MATILDA

TRUMPET

Words and Music by
TIM MINCHIN

WHERE DID THE ROCK GO?

from SCHOOL OF ROCK

TRUMPET

Music by ANDREW LLOYD WEBBER
Lyrics by GLENN SLATER

Your favorite songs are arranged just for solo instrumentalists with this outstanding series. Each book includes great full-accompaniment play-along audio so you can sound just like a pro! Check out **www.halleonard.com** to see all the titles available.

The Beatles

All You Need Is Love • Blackbird • Day Tripper • Eleanor Rigby • Get Back • Here, There and Everywhere • Hey Jude • I Will • Let It Be • Lucy in the Sky with Diamonds • Ob-La-Di, Ob-La-Da • Penny Lane • Something • Ticket to Ride • Yesterday.

_____ 00225330	Flute	$14.99
_____ 00225331	Clarinet	$14.99
_____ 00225332	Alto Sax	$14.99
_____ 00225333	Tenor Sax	$14.99
_____ 00225334	Trumpet.	$14.99
_____ 00225335	Horn	$14.99
_____ 00225336	Trombone	$14.99
_____ 00225337	Violin.	$14.99
_____ 00225338	Viola	$14.99
_____ 00225339	Cello	$14.99

Chart Hits

All About That Bass • All of Me • Happy • Radioactive • Roar • Say Something • Shake It Off • A Sky Full of Stars • Someone like You • Stay with Me • Thinking Out Loud • Uptown Funk.

_____ 00146207	Flute	$12.99
_____ 00146208	Clarinet	$12.99
_____ 00146209	Alto Sax	$12.99
_____ 00146210	Tenor Sax	$12.99
_____ 00146211	Trumpet.	$12.99
_____ 00146212	Horn	$12.99
_____ 00146213	Trombone	$12.99
_____ 00146214	Violin.	$12.99
_____ 00146215	Viola	$12.99
_____ 00146216	Cello	$12.99

Disney Greats

Arabian Nights • Hawaiian Roller Coaster Ride • It's a Small World • Look Through My Eyes • Yo Ho (A Pirate's Life for Me) • and more.

_____ 00841934	Flute	$12.99
_____ 00841935	Clarinet	$12.99
_____ 00841936	Alto Sax	$12.99
_____ 00841937	Tenor Sax	$12.95
_____ 00841938	Trumpet.	$12.99
_____ 00841939	Horn	$12.99
_____ 00841940	Trombone	$12.99
_____ 00841941	Violin.	$12.99
_____ 00841942	Viola	$12.99
_____ 00841943	Cello	$12.99
_____ 00842078	Oboe	$12.99

The Greatest Showman

Come Alive • From Now On • The Greatest Show • A Million Dreams • Never Enough • The Other Side • Rewrite the Stars • This Is Me • Tightrope.

_____ 00277389	Flute	$14.99
_____ 00277390	Clarinet	$14.99
_____ 00277391	Alto Sax	$14.99
_____ 00277392	Tenor Sax	$14.99
_____ 00277393	Trumpet.	$14.99
_____ 00277394	Horn	$14.99
_____ 00277395	Trombone	$14.99
_____ 00277396	Violin.	$14.99
_____ 00277397	Viola	$14.99
_____ 00277398	Cello	$14.99

Movie and TV Music

The Avengers • Doctor Who XI • Downton Abbey • Game of Thrones • Guardians of the Galaxy • Hawaii Five-O • Married Life • Rey's Theme (from *Star Wars: The Force Awakens*) • The X-Files • and more.

_____ 00261807	Flute	$12.99
_____ 00261808	Clarinet	$12.99
_____ 00261809	Alto Sax	$12.99
_____ 00261810	Tenor Sax	$12.99
_____ 00261811	Trumpet.	$12.99
_____ 00261812	Horn	$12.99
_____ 00261813	Trombone	$12.99
_____ 00261814	Violin.	$12.99
_____ 00261815	Viola	$12.99
_____ 00261816	Cello	$12.99

12 Pop Hits

Believer • Can't Stop the Feeling • Despacito • It Ain't Me • Look What You Made Me Do • Million Reasons • Perfect • Send My Love (To Your New Lover) • Shape of You • Slow Hands • Too Good at Goodbyes • What About Us.

_____ 00261790	Flute	$12.99
_____ 00261791	Clarinet	$12.99
_____ 00261792	Alto Sax	$12.99
_____ 00261793	Tenor Sax	$12.99
_____ 00261794	Trumpet.	$12.99
_____ 00261795	Horn	$12.99
_____ 00261796	Trombone	$12.99
_____ 00261797	Violin.	$12.99
_____ 00261798	Viola	$12.99
_____ 00261799	Cello	$12.99

Songs from Frozen, Tangled and Enchanted

Do You Want to Build a Snowman? • For the First Time in Forever • Happy Working Song • I See the Light • In Summer • Let It Go • Mother Knows Best • That's How You Know • True Love's First Kiss • When Will My Life Begin • and more.

_____ 00126921	Flute	$14.99
_____ 00126922	Clarinet	$14.99
_____ 00126923	Alto Sax	$14.99
_____ 00126924	Tenor Sax	$14.99
_____ 00126925	Trumpet.	$14.99
_____ 00126926	Horn	$14.99
_____ 00126927	Trombone	$14.99
_____ 00126928	Violin.	$14.99
_____ 00126929	Viola	$14.99
_____ 00126930	Cello	$14.99

Top Hits

Adventure of a Lifetime • Budapest • Die a Happy Man • Ex's & Oh's • Fight Song • Hello • Let It Go • Love Yourself • One Call Away • Pillowtalk • Stitches • Writing's on the Wall.

_____ 00171073	Flute	$12.99
_____ 00171074	Clarinet	$12.99
_____ 00171075	Alto Sax	$12.99
_____ 00171106	Tenor Sax	$12.99
_____ 00171107	Trumpet.	$12.99
_____ 00171108	Horn	$12.99
_____ 00171109	Trombone	$12.99
_____ 00171110	Violin.	$12.99
_____ 00171111	Viola	$12.99
_____ 00171112	Cello	$12.99

Wicked

As Long As You're Mine • Dancing Through Life • Defying Gravity • For Good • I'm Not That Girl • Popular • The Wizard and I • and more.

_____ 00842236	Flute	$12.99
_____ 00842237	Clarinet	$12.99
_____ 00842238	Alto Saxophone	$12.99
_____ 00842239	Tenor Saxophone.	$11.95
_____ 00842240	Trumpet.	$12.99
_____ 00842241	Horn	$12.99
_____ 00842242	Trombone	$12.99
_____ 00842243	Violin.	$12.99
_____ 00842244	Viola	$12.99
_____ 00842245	Cello	$12.99